GAMES

FOR
ENGLISH AND LANGUAGE ARTS

Charlene Hunter
Isobel L. Livingstone
Bob Loeffelbein
Pat Miller
Cheryl Miller Thurston
Karen Zeinert

Cottonwood Press, Inc.
Fort Collins, Colorado

Requests for permission should be addressed to:

Cottonwood Press, Inc.
109-B Cameron Drive
Fort Collins, Colorado 80525
800-864-4297

ISBN 1-877673-12-9

Printed in the United States of America

Table of Contents

Name _____

Number, Please! **11** *16*

Challenge #1. Each word below contains the letters necessary to spell a number. However, the letters are not always together or in their proper order. For each word, see if you can find the letters that spell a number. The first one is done for you.

1. Snooze _____*one*_____

2. Favorite _____

3. Twine _____

4. Coiffure _____

5. Froze _____

6. Wrote _____

7. Exercise _____

8. Tightest _____

9. Ethereal _____

10. Beginning _____

Challenge #2. For each item below, add the two words together and rearrange the letters so that you can spell out a number. The first one is done for you.

1. tree + thin _____*thirteen*_____

2. vent + yes _____

3. inn + yet _____

4. hit + try _____

Challenge #3. The sentences below contain the letters necessary to spell a number. However, this time the letters you need *are* in order, and the numbers are hidden within words or spread out over several words. Study the sentences carefully and circle the hidden numbers. There are ten numbers in all.

1. I couldn't find a phone that would work.

2. Edith Reed shows real dexterity; she is certainly sleight of hand.

3. Last week I read an exciting book about a Norse venture.

4. That particular story of our past is best forgotten.

5. Dot went yesterday and Leni Nelson left on Friday, but Chef Iverson doesn't plan to leave the restaurant until today.

Challenge #4. See if you can add at least five new items to any one of the challenges above.

14 7 9 **23** 8 5

Answer Key
Number, Please!

Challenge #1
1. one
2. five
3. ten
4. four
5. zero
6. two
7. six
8. eight
9. three
10. nine

Challenge #2
1. thirteen
2. seventy
3. ninety
4. thirty

Challenge #3
1. I couldn't find a ph**one** tha**t wo**uld work.
2. Edi**th Ree**d shows real dexterity; she is certainly sl**eight** of hand.
3. Last week I read an exciting book about a Nor**se ven**ture.
4. That particular story o**f our** past is best forgot**ten**.
5. Do**t went y**esterday and Le**ni Ne**lson left Friday, but Che**f Ive**rson doesn't plan to leave the restaurant until today.

Ik!

Many English words end with an "ik" sound, which can be spelled in different ways. See if you can find the "ik" word that fits each definition below.

1. medicine _____

2. part of a candle _____

3. tiny insect _____

4. top story of some houses _____

5. piece of wood _____

6. material used in building _____

7. action with the foot _____

8. slight wave of the hand _____

9. to imitate _____

10. choose _____

11. cut slightly _____

12. play; have fun _____

13. great _____

14. smooth or slippery _____

15. not thin _____

16. funny _____

17. very worried _____

18. ill _____

19. fast _____

20. humorous, five-lined poem _____

Now make your own puzzle, based upon a different word ending. See if you can think of at least 20 words that end in either "at" or "it." On your own paper, write a puzzle similar to this one, with definitions for each of the 20 words you have chosen.

Answer Key
Ik!

1. tonic
2. wick
3. tick
4. attic
5. stick
6. brick
7. kick
8. flick
9. mimic
10. pick
11. nick
12. frolic
13. terrific
14. slick
15. thick
16. comic
17. frantic
18. sick
19. quick
20. limerick

Disguises

Do you recognize the titles below? They are all the names of common television shows, books or movies — but in disguise. The words have been replaced with synonyms. See if you can "decode" these mysterious titles. (Hint: A thesaurus is the perfect place to discover synonyms.)

1. Bungalow Betterment _____
2. H_2O Child _____
3. Fable About Plaything _____
4. Seedy Roadway _____
5. Prehistoric Recreation Area _____
6. Threatening Apparition _____
7. Disc of Wealth _____
8. Emerald Breakfast Item and Pig Meat _____
9. Celestial Sparkling Flag _____
10. Meteor Conflicts _____
11. Carpet Rodents _____
12. Celebration of 12 Minus 7 _____
13. The Finisher _____
14. Feline Monarch _____
15. Rescued by the Chime _____

Now create ten disguises of your own. Use synonyms to replace the names of television shows, books, movies, musical groups or songs.

Real Name	Disguised Name
1. _____	_____
2. _____	_____
3. _____	_____
4. _____	_____
5. _____	_____
6. _____	_____
7. _____	_____
8. _____	_____
9. _____	_____
10. _____	_____

Answer Key
Disguises

1. Home Improvement
2. The Waterboy
3. Toy Story
4. Sesame Street
5. Jurassic Park
6. The Phantom Menace
7. Wheel of Fortune
8. Green Eggs and Ham
9. Star Spangled Banner
10. Star Wars
11. Rugrats
12. Party of Five
13. The Terminator
14. Lion King
15. Saved by the Bell

Fruits and Vegetables

There are 50 fruits and vegetables hidden below. Unscramble the letters in each item so that you spell the name of the fruit or vegetable. The first one is done for you.

1. chertikoa _____
2. pleap _____
3. ape _____
4. grenoa _____
5. hancips _____
6. prage _____
7. nabana _____
8. slebsurs prustos _____
9. trocar _____
10. brasterwry _____
11. omnel _____
12. iwik _____
13. erbrybeul _____
14. mile _____
15. sperbrary _____
16. nabe _____
17. ronc _____
18. perpep _____
19. shomurom _____
20. totoap _____
21. nonoi _____
22. fragpertui _____
23. reap _____
24. pleapenip _____
25. apacotunel _____

26. lump _____
27. tocnuoc _____
28. ermtawnole _____
29. cobcriol _____
30. saqush _____
31. ewets optoat _____
32. nabe stropu _____
33. chincuzi _____
34. amy _____
35. tead _____
36. surgpaasa _____
37. harbrub _____
38. gacabeb _____
39. cleyer _____
40. yapapa _____
41. bumcucer _____
42. kuppimn _____
43. tripcoa _____
44. shardi _____
45. cheap _____
46. mootat _____
47. ganom _____
48. bekrechuryl _____
49. uprint _____
50. veloi _____

Answer Key
Fruits and Vegetables

1. artichoke
2. apple
3. pea
4. orange
5. spinach
6. grape
7. banana
8. Brussels sprouts
9. carrot
10. strawberry
11. lemon
12. kiwi
13. blueberry
14. lime
15. raspberry
16. bean
17. corn
18. pepper
19. mushroom
20. potato
21. onion
22. grapefruit
23. pear
24. pineapple
25. cantaloupe

26. plum
27. coconut
28. watermelon
29. broccoli
30. squash
31. sweet potato
32. bean sprout
33. zucchini
34. yam
35. date
36. asparagus
37. rhubarb
38. cabbage
39. celery
40. papaya
41. cucumber
42. pumpkin
43. apricot
44. radish
45. peach
46. tomato
47. mango
48. huckleberry
49. turnip
50. olive

Rhyme Time

Part A. Rewrite the phrases below so that each is a two-word rhyme. The first one is done for you, as an example.

1. Thin James _____*slim Jim*_____
2. Depressed father _____
3. Light-colored netting _____
4. High interest _____
5. Cold hammer or saw _____
6. A distant sun _____
7. Illuminated gravel excavation _____
8. Wicked beetle _____
9. An unhappy wildebeest _____
10. A brown panda _____
11. Important show for a rock star _____
12. Smart undertaking _____
13. Sizzling pan _____
14. Reporters driving about, looking for stories _____
15. Overfed Angora _____
16. Small storage area for novels _____
17. Wagnerian opera _____
18. Clever two-winged insect _____
19. An extra piece of fruit _____
20. A big boat _____

Part B. Now add at least five more items of your own to this puzzle, using items 1-20 as models. Be sure to include an answer key on the back of your paper.

Part C. Write a paragraph that includes as many rhyming words as possible. For example, you might begin with something like this:

> *Sue Slew saw a new gnu and a rare bear at the McGoo Zoo on Tuesday morning, a loon at noon, and a wild boar at four.*

Answer Key
Rhyme Time

1. slim Jim
2. sad dad
3. pale veil
4. great rate
5. cool tool
6. far star
7. lit pit
8. evil weevil
9. blue gnu
10. rare bear
11. big gig
12. cleaver endeavor
13. hot pot
14. news cruise
15. fat cat
16. book nook
17. long song
18. sly fly
19. spare pear
20. large barge

Fill the Squares

Using only the names of television shows, see how many squares you can fill in the graph below. These are the rules:

1. Each title must intersect with at least one other title, sharing a letter in common.

2. Titles must read from left to right, or from top to bottom.

3. All words must be spelled correctly.

4. Your goal is to leave as *few* as possible squares empty. When you are finished, you will score one point for each empty box. The object is to get the lowest score possible. Here is an example of how you might start.

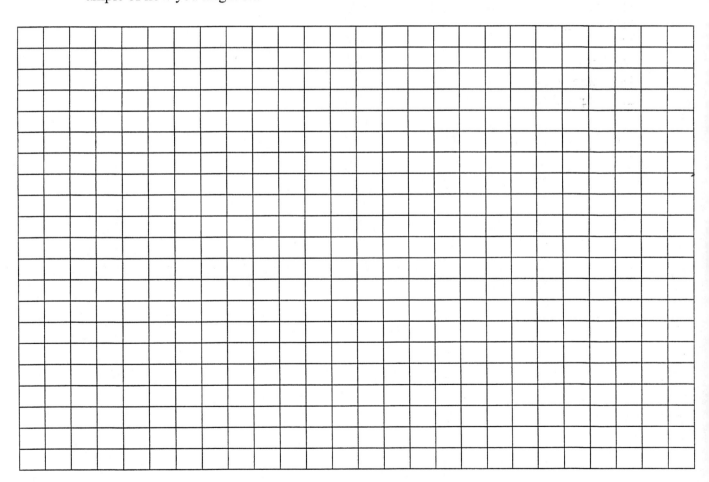

Answer Key
Fill the Squares

Answers will vary. Here is one solution to the puzzle:

		C																					
	C	O	S	B	Y																		
		P						T	H	E	X	F	I	L	E	S			F				
F	R	A	S	I	E	R				E									F	E			D
R			O				P			N									F	L			A
I			S	A	T	U	R	D	A	Y	N	I	G	H	T	L	I	V	E				W
E			S	E			O			A									L	C			S
N		J	A				V			T			P	O	I	R	O	T					O
D	A	T	E	L	I	N	E			I		M		U		P			T				N
S		O					D			D		A		R		A			Y				S
		P	S	E	I	N	F	E	L	D		E		R									C
L	J	A	G							N		A		T									R
A		R		T						C		B	R	A	D	Y	B	U	N	C	H		E
T		D		O						E		O		O									E
E	N	Y	P	D	B	L	U	E				U		F		S	T	A	R	T	R	E	K
N	O		A									T		F									
I	V		M	Y	S	T	E	R	Y			Y			S	I	M	P	S	O	N	S	
G	A											O			V				P				
H												U			E		M	R	B	E	A	N	
T	H	I	S	O	L	D	H	O	U	S	E								A				
								R							7	T	H	H	E	A	V	E	N

Score: 332

Library Scavenger Hunt

"Library Scavenger Hunt" is a challenging and absorbing activity that can be used to help students practice or review library research skills. With this scavenger hunt the students do the work — making up the scavenger hunt list for another team, trying to complete another scavenger hunt list, and checking another team's answers. It's fun to offer a prize of some kind to the winning team, or to every team that scores above a certain number of points. Since the game is a scavenger hunt, it's appropriate that the prizes be "scavenged" prizes. You might bring in garage-sale items yourself, of course. But it's even more fun to have the students bring in scavenger hunt prizes, the sillier the better. They might bring in "white elephants" from their basements, their lockers, garage sales or second-hand stores. Make a big prize table for all the goodies. When it's time for prizes, first-place team winners get first choice, second place team members get second choice, and so on.

"Library Scavenger Hunt" can be varied, of course, for different age and skill levels. The activity takes four to eight class periods, depending upon the amount of time you want the class to spend. Below are day-by-day instructions for the activity:

Orientation/Review
(Two periods or less)

If you are completing the "Library Scavenger Hunt" at the beginning of the school year, allow a day or two to have the librarian give the class a library orientation. If you are completing the activity at the end of the school year, you might want to have a short review of how to use the library.

Introduction and Question Preparation
(Two or three periods)

Before class begins, fill in some interesting topics for items 23-25 on "Categories for the Library Scavenger Hunt" (page 22). Have some fun with this one, choosing very specific topics of all kinds, from important to oddball. For example, you might choose *Luke Perry, crocodiles,* and *polo* for one instruction sheet. Another might include *Ivan the Terrible,* the *accordion,* and the planet *Neptune.* Make sure the topics are ones that students will be able to find in the library.

Divide your class into teams of three or four students each, giving each team a copy of the team instructions for "Library Scavenger Hunt" (page 21) and "Categories for the Library Scavenger Hunt" (page 22). Go over the instructions with the students. Then take them to the library and let them begin work.

At the end of the allotted time, collect a list of scavenger hunt questions from each group, along with an accompanying answer sheet. Scan the questions to be sure all the questions are suitable. (If you have been monitoring the groups as they work, this step won't be so important. Don't worry too much if every question isn't clear. Students may be a lot more receptive, after struggling with imprecise questions, to a follow-up lesson or discussion about writing clearly.)

The Scavenger Hunt
(One or two periods)

Give every team a new list of scavenger hunt questions — in other words, a list *other* than the one the group prepared. Explain that students have the next one (or two) periods to complete as many of the scavenger hunt questions as possible. Then turn them loose in the library.

Checking
(One period)

Give each team's scavenger hunt answer sheet to the team that originally prepared the questions. Have each team use the answer sheet it originally prepared to check the answers and come up with a final score, allowing four points per correct answer, with two points for answers that are partially correct. (Before checking begins, it's a good idea to talk about being reasonable. For example, if the correct answer is the color "scarlet," a team should count "red" or "ruby" as correct. If the correct answer is "in a lake," the team should also allow credit for answers like "in a large body of water.")

When the team has finished scoring a paper, the paper should be given back to the team who completed it, with the answer sheet, to see if there are objections to any of the decisions in checking. Allow time to handle any disputes, and then post the final scores for each team.

Finally, award your "scavenged" prizes.

Library Scavenger Hunt

With this scavenger hunt, your team will play two roles. First, you will be the "writers," creating a scavenger hunt question list for another team to complete. Then you will act as "hunters," completing a scavenger hunt question list created by another team.

It is important that your team members work together, that you are accurate in your work, and that you follow directions carefully. Here are the steps you will follow:

Orientation/Review

Your class will learn about the library — or review what you have already learned.

Preparing Questions

Your team will write 25 questions for another team to answer later on. However, these can't be just any questions. They must fit the categories on the next page, and they must be typed or copied neatly. You must also prepare a separate answer sheet. The answer sheet must include the exact place where each answer can be found.

Example

Answer: Thailand (*1994 Information Please Almanac,* page 270).

The Scavenger Hunt

Your team will receive a list of questions from another team. Your task will be to answer correctly as many questions as possible in the time allowed, using the library. The winning group will be the group that answers the most questions correctly.

Name _____

Categories for the
Library Scavenger Hunt

1. A question that can be answered by using the card catalog (or computer)

2. A question that can be answered by using an unabridged dictionary or a specialized dictionary

3. A question that can be answered by using an encyclopedia

4. A question that can be answered by using an almanac

5. A question that can be answered by using an atlas

6. A question that can be answered by using a biographical reference book

7. A question that can be answered by using a magazine

8. A question that can be answered by using the Internet

9. A question about geography

10. A question about art

11. A question about music

12. A question about movies

13. A question about history

14. A question about nature

15. A question about an author

16. A question about sports

17. A question about a famous person

18. A question about any subject that begins with the letter *m*

19. A question about the Bill of Rights

20. A question about an animal

21. A question about a war

22. A question about a food

23. A question about _____

24. A question about _____

25. A question about _____

Scrambles

Each box below contains scrambled letters. The letters in each box can be arranged and rearranged to spell four different words. See if you can find all of them.

T E D I	_ _ _ _
	_ _ _ _
	_ _ _ _
	_ _ _ _

_ _ _ _	I E T M
_ _ _ _	
_ _ _ _	
_ _ _ _	

P S N I	_ _ _ _
	_ _ _ _
	_ _ _ _
	_ _ _ _

_ _ _ _	E T S A
_ _ _ _	
_ _ _ _	
_ _ _ _	

Make some scrambles of your own, below:

	_ _ _ _
	_ _ _ _
	_ _ _ _
	_ _ _ _

_ _ _ _	
_ _ _ _	
_ _ _ _	
_ _ _ _	

	_ _ _ _
	_ _ _ _
	_ _ _ _
	_ _ _ _

_ _ _ _	
_ _ _ _	
_ _ _ _	
_ _ _ _	

Answer Key
Scrambles

diet
edit
tide
tied

spin
pins
snip
nips

time
mite
emit
item

east
seat
teas
eats

Bill Cosby Meets the Slimy Rubber Band Monster in the Center of Mom's Microwave

For a Halloween writing challenge, try having students write fill-in-the-blank paragraphs. First, have each student write down, on a slip of paper, an item that fits each of the following categories:

1. The name of a person — someone famous or someone known to the class.

2. An interesting adjective that could be used in front of the word *monster*. (Examples: specific words like *wart-covered* and *slippery*, rather than general words like *ugly* and *scary*.)

3. A specific, interesting noun. (Examples: *kitchen faucet, shoestrings, dust bunnies,* rather than *boy* or *clothes.*)

4. A specific place in your city or town. (Example: *on the drain at the bottom of the swimming pool*, rather than just *the pool.*)

    (Note: It is a good idea to mention that all words should, of course, be appropriate for class. Having students put their names on the papers also helps guard against inappropriate language.)

Now, have the students pass in their slips of paper. Place all the slips in a paper bag. Explain that each row of students will receive a different assignment, according to the slips of paper drawn out of the bag. Then begin drawing. Choose a #1 item from the first slip, a #2 item from the second, and so forth, until the first row has a set of four different items. List the items on the board, and then begin drawing for the next row.

When each row has a list of four items, you can explain what the students are going to do with their designated lists. They are to write a descriptive paragraph or two (you set the limits) on this topic: (Item #1) meets the (Item #2) (Item #3) Monster at (Item #4). For example, one result might be this: Bill Cosby meets the slimy Rubber Band Monster in the center of Mom's microwave.

In other words, students will be writing a description of a meeting between a person and a monster at a designated place. Of course, the paragraphs may have to be fairly outlandish in order to incorporate what may be some bizarre characters and circumstances, but that's all right. Part of the fun is the challenge of this assignment.

Sharing results is very important. One effective method is to have each row meet as a group to share paragraphs. The students can then choose the one or two papers they would most like the rest of the class to hear.

Questions, Questions

We are all used to answering questions — or trying to. For a change of pace, try coming up with the questions instead of the answers. Be creative as you think of three questions you could ask to receive each answer below.

Example

The answer is *disgusting*.

The questions are:

- How do you describe a piece of lasagna that sat, forgotten, in a plastic container at the back of the refrigerator for two months?
- What word describes the frog I had to dissect in biology class?
- How does my mother describe the state of my room whenever she has to go near it?

1. The answer is *empty*.

2. The answer is *red*.

3. The answer is *scratchy*.

4. The answer is *puppy*.

5. The answer is *tired*.

6. The answer is *wonderful*.

7. The answer is *commercials*.

8. The answer is *friends*.

9. The answer is *not on your life*.

10. The answer is *questions*.

Answer Key
Questions, Questions

Answers will vary. Here are some possibilities:

1. How does my stomach feel during second period math class?
   How did I feel when my best friend moved away?
   How do you describe an airhead's brain?

2. How do you describe Jack's face when the teacher read the love note he was sending to Katy?
   What did I see when my brother told me he ripped my favorite sweater?
   What color did you turn in church when someone made an embarrassing noise and you were trying not to laugh?

3. How do my mom's old Neil Diamond records sound?
   What kind of throat makes you want to grab a cup of hot tea?
   How do chicken pox make you feel?

4. Happiness is a warm what?
   What makes me smile as soon as I open the door at home after school?
   How does my mom describe the love I feel for Allison?

5. How do you feel after listening to your Aunt Martha tell about her Tupperware party, again?
   What describes a car with wheels on it?
   How do you feel immediately upon hearing that someone needs help with the dishes?

6. What is a snow day?
   How does your favorite T-shirt feel when you take it out of the dryer?
   What word would you like to see at the top of your report, instead of "needs work"?

7. What makes your thumb start moving on the remote control?
   What do you wish wouldn't include embarrassing subjects when you are watching T.V. with members of the opposite sex?
   What makes you wish you had an unlimited supply of money?

8. Who can you count on to stand by you through thick or thin?
   Who doesn't laugh (at least much!) when you drop chocolate pudding in your lap?
   Who sometimes gets you in trouble when they sit too close to you in class?

9. Do you prefer fat free peach yogurt to Haagen-Daz chocolate fudge swirl?
   Would your mom let you have a pet boa constrictor?
   Wouldn't you like your parents to be the chaperones for the school dance?

10. What do my parents give me before and after I go to a party?
    What can you count on getting from your teacher if your mind wanders during class?
    What do little kids never run out of?

Alphabet Trade Names

1. Begin writing the letters of the alphabet down the left-hand side of a piece of paper, skipping a couple of lines after each letter. When you run out of room, continue to a new sheet of paper. When you have the entire alphabet written, you are ready to begin the game.

2. The object of the game is to find trade names that begin with each letter of the alphabet. What is a trade name? It is the *commercial* name of a product, or of the company that makes the product. For example, "Fruit Loops" is a trade name, and so is "Kellogg," the name of the company that makes the cereal. However, "corn flakes" and "oatmeal" are not trade names.

    When you think of a trade name that begins with a certain letter, write that trade name beside the appropriate letter. For example, you could write "Fruit Loops" beside the "F" or "Kellogg" beside the "K." (Don't use these two examples, though. You will need to think of your own.)

3. When you have one trade name for each letter, A-Z, you have completed the basics of the game — almost. There is one more requirement: You must be sure that you have included at least one trade name from each of the categories below:

medicines	*beauty products*	*candy bars*
cars	*soaps*	*cereals*
appliances	*toys or games*	*things to wear*
pet foods		

4. When you finish the basics, you have earned 50 points. Then you may go on to earn bonus points by thinking of *more* than one trade name for each letter. You will receive one bonus point for each extra trade name you write down. See if you or your group can earn the highest score in the time allotted.

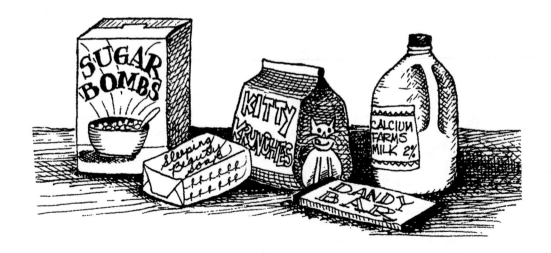

Answer Key
Alphabet Trade Names

Answers will vary. Here are some possibilities:

Advil
Bayer
Coca-Cola
Doc Martens
Energizer
Frosted Flakes
Gerber
Hershey
Ivory
Jergens
Kleenex
Luvs
Maytag
Nissan
Oil of Olay
Purina
Quaker State Motor Oil
Rolaids
Scrabble
Tide
United Airlines
Vaseline
Woolite
Xerox
Yellow Freight
Zenith

Xtra! Xtra!

Part A

The words defined below all contain the letter *x*. Following the definitions is an "X Word Bank" that includes all of the answers, plus many other *x* words. Study the list carefully to select the best word for each definition. Draw a line through each word in the word bank as you use it.

1. to show _____

2. wind instrument _____

3. to surpass _____

4. a bleach _____

5. to confuse _____

6. smoked salmon _____

7. harmful to health _____

8. colorless gas _____

9. dictionary _____

10. to give and receive _____

11. two identical parts under one roof _____

12. to leave out _____

X Word Bank

approximate	axes	boxing	complex
duplex	exalt	exams	exceed
exchange	exclude	exert	exhibit
exist	index	lexicon	lox
maximum	next	noxious	oxen
oxygen	peroxide	perplex	plexus
proxy	quixotic	saxophone	sixty
taxes	vixen	xylophone	

Part B

The answers to the words defined below can also be found in the "X Word Bank." However, you must do some revising. Study the words you *haven't* used. By dropping an *x* and rearranging the remaining letters, you will find the answers. The first one is done for you as an example.

1. number _____
2. period of time _____
3. location _____
4. body of water _____
5. alike _____

6. a story _____
7. bench, chair _____
8. to eat _____
9. climbing plant _____
10. pine, for example _____

Part C

See if you can recall some names spelled with an *x*.

1. a former U.S. President _____
2. a baseball team _____
3. popular elasticized fabric _____
4. a girl's name _____
5. two states _____

Part D

In the space below, see if you can add five more items to the Part C exercise.

Answer Key
Xtra! Xtra!

Part A
1. exhibit
2. saxophone
3. exceed
4. peroxide
5. perplex
6. lox
7. noxious
8. oxygen
9. lexicon
10. exchange
11. duplex
12. exclude

Part B
1. ten (next)
2. eon (oxen)
3. site (exist)
4. sea (axes)
5. same (exams)
6. tale (exalt)
7. seat (taxes)
8. dine (index)
9. vine (vixen)
10. tree (exert)

Part C
1. Richard Nixon
2. White Sox or Red Sox
3. spandex
4. Maxine
5. Texas, New Mexico

Those Disagreeable G's

Have you ever noticed how many sometimes-unpleasant words begin with *G*? Using the definitions that follow, see if you can complete the *G* words below. When you have the puzzle completed correctly, the boxed letters will spell out the name of a Halloween song.

1. _____ me with a spoon!   G _ _

2. Member of a group of criminals.   G _ _ _ _ _ _ _

3. Blood and _____   G _ O _

4. It haunts.   G O _ _ _

5. Selfish; wanting it all.   G _ _ O _

6. Grit and _____   G _ _ O _

7. A frame for hanging criminals.   G _ _ _ O _ _

8. Often thrown at the enemy during war.   G _ _ O _ _ _

9. A word teenagers use to describe anything they don't like.   G _ _ O _

10. Someone who makes a pig of himself or herself.   G _ _ _ O _ _

11. Horrible; repulsive.   G _ _ O _ _ _

12. Something people hate to take out.   G _ O _ _ _ _

13. A *gnome* that causes things to go wrong.   G _ _ O _ _ _

14. What a vampire won't stay in.   G _ O _ _

16. What someone might do if confronted by King Kong.   G _ O _

16. A knife might make one.   G _ _ O

17. It shoots.   G _ _

18. Crabby or cranky.   G _ _ _ _ _

19. You might have to have a leg cut off if this sets in.   G _ _ _ _ _ _

20. It cuts off heads.   G _ _ _ _ _ _ _

The Halloween Song is

___ ___ ___   ___ ___ ___ ___ ___ ___ ___   ___ ___ ___

Answer Key
Those Disagreeable G's

1. GAG
2. GANGSTER
3. GUTS
4. GHOST
5. GREEDY
6. GRIME
7. GALLOWS
8. GRENADE
9. GROSS
10. GLUTTON
11. GRUESOME
12. GARBAGE
13. GREMLIN
14. GRAVE
15. GASP
16. GASH
17. GUN
18. GROUCHY
19. GANGRENE
20. GUILLOTINE

The Halloween Song is "The Monster Mash."

Winter

Directions:

Make up categories and list them along the left side of the game, in the boxes provided. You may choose any categories at all that are appropriate for class. (Examples: cartoon characters, six-letter words, things that are sweet, etc.) Be creative in choosing your categories!

For each category along the left, think of an appropriate item that *begins* with the letter at the top of the column. Then think of an item from that category that *ends* with the letter at the top of the column. Score one point for each item you correctly fill in.

The first line is completed for you, as an example.

Category	W	I	N	T	E	R	Score
Colors	white yellow	indigo kiwi	nude brown	teal violet	ecru periwinkle	red umber	12

Total Score _____

Answer Key
Winter

Answers will vary. Here is one possible solution:

Category	W	I	N	T	E	R	Score
Fruits	water-melon honeydew	Italian tomato kiwi	nectarine lemon	tangerine apricot	elderberry lime	raspberry pear	12
Sandwich Fixin's	watercress coleslaw	ice cream pepperoni	nuts chicken	tomato liverwurst	eggs cheese	roast beef butter	12
Musical Instruments	whistle saw	idiophone timpani	Nickelodeon accordion	trumpet clarinet	electric guitar oboe	recorder guitar	12
Ice Cream Flavors	Wavy Gravy marshmallow	Irish Crème spumoni	Neapolitan butter pecan	tin roof peppermint	English toffee chocolate	rocky road rootbeer	12
Things to Wear	watch bow	ice skate bikini	nylons pin	T-shirt bracelet	earrings necklace	ring sweater	12
Types of Dogs	Weimaraner chow	Irish setter Shar-Pei	Newfoundland Dalmatian	terrier mutt	English setter collie	rottweiler schnauzer	12
Cities	Walla Walla Barrow	Indianapolis Cotaxi	North Fork Jackson	Toledo Flint	Everett Rifle	Richmond Sweetwater	12
5-Letter Names	Wally Turow	Isaac Patti	Nancy Susan	Trina Trent	Ethan Marie	Ralph Tyler	12

Total Score ___96___

Diamond Stories

See if you can write a short story in diamond form. The first line of the story should consist of one word, the second line of two words, the third line of three words, and so on. Each line should be a complete sentence.

Continue until you have reached at least ten or eleven words in a line. Then begin to shorten your lines, one word at a time, until you have only one word left.

Here is an example of a diamond story:

"Stop!"

Bill froze.

"Who goes there?"

"Bill Jacobs Johnson, sir."

"You're supposed to be inside!"

"I understand that, sir, but I . . . ."

"Don't you obey the rules around here?"

"Yes, but I'm on an important mission, sir."

"What kind of mission would have you sneaking about?"

"Well, sir it's a . . . it's a mercy mission, top secret."

"I've heard that before," the officer said, pulling out his wallet.

Bill stared at the officer when he handed him money.

"Bill, you are on the *usual* mercy mission, right?"

"I don't think I should say more, sir."

"Aren't you going to town for pizzas?"

"I didn't know you knew about . . . ."

"We have awful grub, Bill."

Bill smiled. "Your order?"

"Make mine pepperoni."

"Yes, sir!"

"Go!"

Name_____

A+

All clues below identify a word that has at least one *a* in it. The first letter is provided for you. See if you can fill in the blanks.

1. letters   A __ __ __ __ __ __ __
2. fruit   B __ __ __ __ __
3. flower   C __ __ __ __ __ __ __ __
4. gemstone   D __ __ __ __ __ __
5. animal   E __ __ __ __ __ __ __
6. story   F __ __ __ __
7. wager   G __ __ __ __ __
8. hinder   H __ __ __ __ __ __
9. question   I __ __ __ __ __ __ __ __ __ __
10. wild dog   J __ __ __ __ __
11. animal   K __ __ __ __ __ __ __
12. smallest   L __ __ __ __
13. keep up   M __ __ __ __ __ __ __
14. country   N __ __ __ __ __
15. musical   O __ __ __ __
16. food   P __ __ __ __
17. bird   Q __ __ __ __
18. contest   R __ __ __
19. Iowa, Texas   S __ __ __ __ __
20. late   T __ __ __ __
21. used for rain   U __ __ __ __ __ __ __
22. holiday   V __ __ __ __ __ __ __ __
23. rich   W __ __ __ __ __ __
24. uses radiation   X __ __ __
25. 52 weeks   Y __ __ __
26. silly   Z __ __ __

Answer Key
A+

1. alphabet
2. banana
3. carnation
4. diamond
5. elephant
6. fable
7. gamble
8. hamper
9. interrogate
10. jackal
11. kangaroo
12. least
13. maintain
14. nation
15. opera
16. pizza
17. quail
18. race
19. states
20. tardy
21. umbrella
22. vacation
23. wealthy
24. x-ray
25. year
26. zany

Name _____

Thanksgiving

There are many words hidden in the word *Thanksgiving*. See if you can find a word that fits each definition below. Remember, you may use only the letters in *Thanksgiving* for your answers.

1. What Jack Sprat's wife was not _____

2. The opposite of *that* _____

3. Precedes *you* in a kind of note you must write after Christmas _____

4. Another name for a witch_____

5. Children often do this by their knees at recess_____

6. A helping verb _____

7. Opposite of *hers* _____

8. What your mother says you should never do to your brother_____

9. A bald person often likes to wear one _____

10. What you drop when Christmas or a birthday is coming up _____

11. In the olden days, naughty boys often dipped pigtails in this _____

12. They love picnics _____

13. What you should do before you borrow your brother's favorite sweater _____

14. You probably feel that your parents and teachers do this to you _____

15. Relatives_____

16. What a skunk does _____

17. What your teacher wants you to do when you come into the room _____

18. A kind of carpet that needs raking _____

19. You never want to commit one of these_____

20. You can carry a lot of stuff if you drive one of these_____

21. Several people might act in one of these _____

22. If you didn't have this, your insides would fall out _____

23. What the kids did when the birthday cake was brought out_____

24. It might have a name like *Sharks* or *Bruisers* _____

25. Your teachers and parents always tell you to do this before you act _____

26. Cars need it_____

27. Ant bites do this _____

28. The Titanic did this _____

Now see if you can find five more words hidden in the word *Thanksgiving*, and write definitions for them. See if other class members can find the answers to *your* definitions.

Answer Key
Thanksgiving

1. thin
2. this
3. thank
4. hag
5. hang
6. is (or has)
7. his
8. hit
9. hat
10. hint
11. ink
12. ants
13. ask
14. nag
15. kin
16. stink
17. sit
18. shag
19. sin
20. van
21. skit
22. skin
23. sang
24. gang
25. think
26. gas
27. sting
28. sank

Changing Around

One word in each item below is in capital letters. Change one letter in that word (and switch letters about, if needed) to fill in the second blank. Then change another letter in order to fill in the third blank.

Example

Last spring, it was **COLD** and damp, and patches of __ __ __ __ began to appear on the ground, even on well-drained __ __ __ __ . It was so cold and damp that it was unpleasant to __ __ __ __ about the grounds.

1. I just **LOVE** Mark's tall tales. He was the one who told us about the woman who discovered a major __ __ __ __ of __ __ __ __ on his grandfather's ranch. Although I didn't believe him, it was a __ __ __ __ story.

2. Bill **FARE** shouted __ __ __ __! No one reacted, though, because he has paid a __ __ __ __ every year for the last __ __ __ __ years for doing the same thing. He has an overactive imagination.

3. Justin is **NEAT**. He is a good student and a __ __ __ __ captain. He's also very responsible, even in his social life. For example, he has never once been __ __ __ __ for a __ __ __ __.

4. Katie is not a very good **COOK**, but she always looks __ __ __ __, even when things aren't going well. Once she used a pile of real __ __ __ __ instead of charcoal. The fire got so hot, she singed the __ __ __ __ on her collar. She kept smiling, though.

5. Sara likes to **SING**. She gets a big __ __ __ __ on her face whenever she gets the opportunity to perform. Sometimes when she walks down the hall at school, she bursts into song. Her embarrassed friends say, "Please get a __ __ __ __ on yourself!" Sara won't listen, though. Her friends just have to __ __ __ __ their teeth and put up with her outbursts.

Now add five items of your own to this puzzle. You may start with any words that you like, but here are some suggestions: *mist, brat, robe, drum, goat, hill, sack, pest, wars.*

Answer Key
Changing Around

1. LOVE, lode, gold, good
2. FARE, fire, fine, five (or nine)
3. NEAT, team, late, date
4. COOK, cool, coal, lace
5. SING, grin, grip, grit

One Step at a Time

To answer each question below, follow the instructions below it very carefully, one step at a time. If you follow the instructions precisely, you will be able to write the answer to each question in the space provided.

A. Question:

What do you call a lion who chases camels across the desert?

Answer: _____

SAM AND YOLANDA READ ABOUT SCALAWAGS

1. Look at the sentence written in capital letters above. Cross out all the letters except the first in each proper name.

2. Cross out the word that can be pronounced two different ways.

3. Cross out the word that contains the first and second letters of the alphabet.

4. Cross out the first, third, seventh and eighth letters in the longest word.

5. The letters that are left spell the answer to the question above. Print them in the space provided.

B. Question:

What English word has the most letters?

Answer: _____

GAIL FREDERICKS BOUGHT BOB AN OX.

1. Look at the sentence written in capital letters above. Cross out the first two-letter word.

2. Cross out the longest proper noun.

3. Cross out the shortest proper noun.

4. Cross out all letters except the first in the verb.

5. Change the G in the girl's name to the thirteenth letter of the alphabet.

6. The letters that are left spell the answer to the question. Print them on the spaces provided.

C. Question:

What gift made the bald man exclaim, "I'll never part with it"?

Answer: _____

MR. GLOCK INSTALLED A COMBINATION LOCK ON MY LOCKER.

1. Look at the sentence written in capital letters above. Cross out the two rhyming words.

2. Cross out the word in past tense.

3. Cross out the abbreviation.

4. Cross out the prepositional phrase.

5. Cross out the last seven letters in the four-syllable word.

6. The letters that are left spell the answer to the question. Print them in the space provided.

D. Challenge.

See if you can construct your own one-step-at-a-time puzzle, building the puzzle around a riddle of your choice. Warning: This will not be an easy task!

Answer Key
One Step at a Time

A. Sandy Claws
B. Mailbox
C. A comb
D. Answers will vary

Holiday Anagrams

There are 40 terms associated with the holidays hidden below. Unscramble the letters in each item so that you spell a holiday word (or words). The first item is done for you. (Note: the items with stars have answers of two or more words.)

1. stifg _____
2. direrene _____
3. lohyl _____
4. sgakpace _____
5. arthew _____
6. anlutscasa ★ _____
7. gicksnot _____
8. incragol _____
9. evraysweene ★ _____
10. unslotsoire _____
11. novatica _____
12. shetramstrice ★ _____
13. tremanson _____
14. polrhud _____
15. snetli _____
16. toilteems _____
17. gliths _____
18. snestrep _____
19. lopethorn ★ _____
20. geggon _____

21. slelb _____
22. wlefaksons _____
23. yetruk _____
24. skoicoe _____
25. gilhes _____
26. ringecradtge ★ _____
27. inbrob _____
28. swob _____
29. veels _____
30. capetinemime ★ _____
31. grishan _____
32. erd _____
33. teerapreetgrainridap ★ _____
34. ecape _____
35. dayaccnen ★ _____
36. otintapies _____
37. splugrumas ★ _____
38. ogresco _____
39. gnere _____
40. veergeren _____

Answer Key
Holiday Anagrams

1. gifts
2. reindeer
3. holly
4. packages
5. wreath
6. Santa Claus
7. stocking
8. caroling
9. New Year's Eve
10. resolutions
11. vacation
12. Christmas tree
13. ornaments
14. Rudolph
15. tinsel
16. mistletoe
17. lights
18. presents
19. North Pole
20. eggnog

21. bells
22. snowflakes
23. turkey
24. cookies
25. sleigh
26. greeting card
27. ribbon
28. bows
29. elves
30. mincemeat pie
31. sharing
32. red
33. partridge in a pear tree
34. peace
35. candy cane
36. poinsettia
37. sugar plums
38. Scrooge
39. green
40. evergreen

Ded Cat

Directions:

As you rewrite *Ded Cat*, see if you can find and correct all 79 spelling errors.

Ded Cat

An urbun ledgend is a storie told over and over, in many diffrent forms, all over the countrey — or even the wourld. Peopel tell the story, beleiving it to be ture, but know one has ever been able to track down the acshual peopel involved. The storie always hapened to "my best freind's brother's ex-grilfreind" or to "a freind of my mother's boss," or to "a freind of a freind." Here is one vershun of an urbun ledgend called "Ded Cat":

A man and a women went shoping together, and the man desided to by his wife the beauteful blowse she fell in love with at an expensive store. She was thrilled, hapily carring the blowse to the car in the bag provided by the store.

Then the cuple desided to stop at a restraunt too eat. They got out of there car and started to go inside, but then they saw a ded cat in the parcking lot.

"Oh deer," said the women. "We can't just leave the pore thing there. Someone might run over it again."

The man agreed. They were both cat lovers and thouhgt the aminal decerved a desent berial. He thought a moment, then took the blowse out of the bag from the expensive store and replaced it with the ded cat. Then he put the bag on the hood of the car while he and his wife went in to eat. They planned to take the ded cat home with them later and bery it.

Another women walking passed the car saw the bag on the hood. Quikly, she looked around to see if anywone was looking. Then she picked up the bag and casualy caried it into the restraunt. She ordered a ham and cheeze samwich and sat down to eat.

Curiousity got the best of her, and finly she desided to peek inside the bag. When se saw the ded cat, she fainted.

The maneger caled an ambulanse and help soon arived. The ambulanse atendents put the women on a strecher, along with her purse. As she was being loded up into the ambulanse, the bag contaning the ded cat sat on her stomack.

Answer Key
The Ded Cat

Dead Cat

(24) An **urban legend** is a **story** told over and over, in many **different** forms, all over the **country** — or even the **world**. **People** tell the story, **believing** it to be **true**, but **no** one has ever been able to track down the **actual people** involved. The **story** always **happened** to "my best **friend's** brother's **ex-girlfriend**" or to "a **friend** of my mother's boss," or to "a **friend** of a **friend**." Here is one **version** of an **urban legend** called "**Dead** Cat":

(9) A man and a **woman** went **shopping** together, and the man **decided** to **buy** his wife the **beautiful blouse** she fell in love with at an expensive store. She was thrilled, **happily carrying** the **blouse** to the car in the bag provided by the store.

(1) Then the **couple decided** to stop at a **restaurant to** eat. They got out of **their** car and started to go inside, but then they saw a **dead** cat in the **parking** lot.

(3) "Oh **dear**," said the **woman**. "We can't just leave the **poor** thing there. Someone might run over it again."

(9) The man agreed. They were both cat lovers and **thought** the **animal deserved** a **decent burial**. He thought a moment, then took the **blouse** out of the bag from the expensive store and replaced it with the **dead** cat. Then he put the bag on the hood of the car while he and his wife went in to eat. They planned to take the **dead** cat home with them later and **bury** it.

(9) Another **woman** walking **past** the car saw the bag on the hood. **Quickly**, she looked around to see if **anyone** was looking. Then she picked up the bag and **casually carried** it into the **restaurant**. She ordered a ham and **cheese sandwich** and sat down to eat.

(5) **Curiosity** got the best of her, and **finally** she **decided** to peek inside the bag. When **she** saw the **dead** cat, she fainted.

(13) The **manager called** an **ambulance**, and help soon **arrived**. The **ambulance attendants** put the **woman** on a **stretcher**, along with her purse. As she was being **loaded** up into the **ambulance**, the bag **containing** the **dead** cat sat on her **stomach**.

Nouns, Nouns, Everywhere Nouns

The short paragraph below contains twenty nouns. One of them has been written in bold and also copied into the puzzle grid. See if you can find and circle the rest of the nouns in the paragraph; then put all of the nouns in their proper places in the grid. (Hint: Putting the words in their proper places in the grid is not as easy as it looks!)

Marcy liked pizza. In fact, it was her favorite snack. She liked thick **crusts** better than the thin and crispy type, but she wasn't really fussy. She would eat either kind if it had big gobs of cheese. She always ordered extra toppings, like pepperoni, Italian sausage, black olives, green peppers, onions and mushrooms. She usually washed the whole thing down with a quart of pop. She had a big appetite!

Answer Key
Nouns, Nouns, Everywhere Nouns

Marcy liked *pizza*. In *fact*, it was her favorite *snack*. She liked thick *crusts* better than the thin and crispy *type*, but she wasn't really fussy. She would eat either *kind* if it had big *gobs* of *cheese*. She always ordered extra *toppings*, like *pepperoni,* Italian *sausage*, black *olives*, green *peppers*, *onions* and *mushrooms*. She usually washed the whole *thing* down with a *quart* of *pop*. She had a big *appetite*!

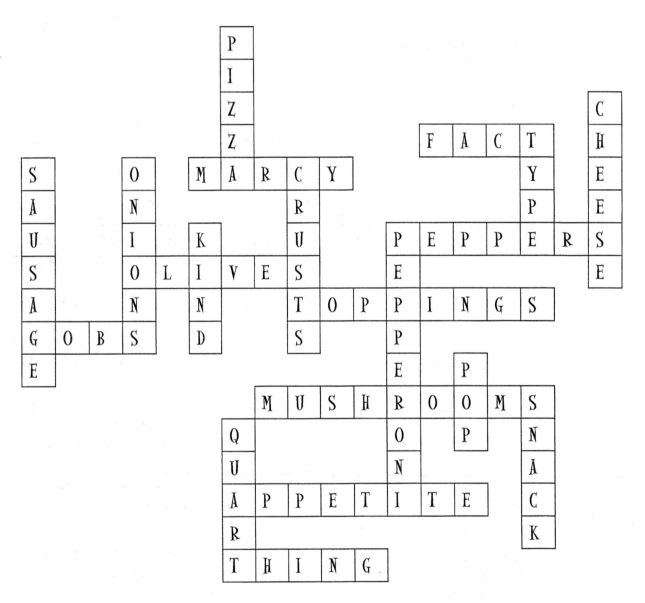

Martians vs. Earthlings

"Martians vs. Earthlings" is a game that is perfect for the last month of school. It is active, yet it has the very attractive feature (to teachers!) of requiring silence from most players. It takes thinking, creativity and ingenuity on the part of the students. It also involves communication — though of the non-verbal kind. With luck, the game may even give students more appreciation for the role language plays in our world.

Materials

You will need a timer, one that rings, beeps, buzzes or makes some other kind of noise. You will also need to prepare some flash cards ahead of time. A list of possible topics for the cards is on the next page.

Playing the Game

When students come into class, have them draw numbers that designate them as Martians, Earthlings or Zelbotians Rulers. There should be only four or five Zelbotians Rulers, with the rest of the class divided equally between Martians and Earthlings. Thus, a class of 35 might have five Zelbotians Rulers, 15 Earthlings and 15 Martians.

Explain that a space-traveling team of Earthlings and a space-traveling team of Martians have simultaneously had mechanical difficulties and landed on an unknown planet, a planet that has room for only one more group of beings. The planet's Zelbotians Rulers must decide which group to allow to stay and which group to toss back into outer space — a very dangerous alternative.

The Zelbotians Rulers have decided to keep the group that proves itself to be the best at communicating. However, there's a problem. The Zelbotians Rulers understand neither Martian nor English and, in fact, become quite irritated by the sound of either language. The Martians and Earthlings must find ways to communicate without using language, according to the following test:

- The teams will take turns trying to communicate the meaning of different words on flashcards to the Zelbotians Rulers. The teams must communicate with each other and with the Zelbotians Rulers entirely *without* using spoken or written language.

- Because the Zelbotians Rulers hate the sound of languages they don't understand, the Earthlings will lose a point every time anyone in their group speaks, and the Martians will lose a point every time any Martian speaks. The same goes for any kind of written communication.

- The Zelbotians Rulers will flip a coin to see which team goes first. Then, the designated card holder (the teacher) will hold up a flash card to that team. That team will have one minute to try to communicate the word to the Zelbotians Rulers.

For example, if the flashcard says "love," the team members will do all they can to get the Zelbotians Rulers to say "love." If the Zelbotians Rulers guess the correct word before the timer sounds, the communicating team will gain one point.

Yes, the Zelbotians Rulers get to speak. Their scientists have developed a device called the *transmitifier*, which allows their language to be understood by anyone who hears it, no matter what the person's native language. Thus the Martians will hear what the Zelbotians Rulers say as Martian, and the Earthlings will hear whatever the Zelbotians Rulers say as English.

The Earthlings and Martians can't use language at all, even to communicate with each other. Therefore, they may find it difficult to determine how to proceed in trying to communicate a word to the Zelbotians Rulers. It will take cooperation and creativity for a group to work together effectively.

- At the end of one minute, play goes to the next team. The card holder holds up a new card, and then the new team has one minute to communicate the word to the Zelbotians Rulers.

- Points are kept, even when a team goes into negative numbers. If a team has 0 points and someone speaks, the team will then have minus 1 point.

Possible Topics
love • hamburgers • taste • smell • ice flower •
motorcycle • intelligence • hot
slow • hammer • book • words • green
newspaper • umbrella • television
telephone • numbers • beautiful • star
water • fish • calculator • sky • impatience
penguin • yellow • mother • temperature
paper • drew • carpet • cat • shy • milk
rain • skyscraper • rainbow • bus
envelope • talk • brave • ocean • hope

Lipograms

Lipograms are sentences that do not contain a particular letter of the alphabet. Create some lipograms by rewriting the sentences below.

Eliminate all the *a*'s in Sentence #1, the *b*'s in Sentence #2, and the *c*'s in Sentence #3. In rewriting the sentences you may substitute words, add words, or subtract words. However, you may not alter the basic meaning to the sentence.

Example

Create a lipogram by rewriting the following sentence to eliminate the letter *t*:

Robert really liked to read cartoons on Saturday and Sunday mornings.

Bob loved reading comics on weekend mornings

Sentence #1
(Eliminate the letter *a*.)

Richard adored the food of France, and he ate custards or pastries regularly while he was there.

_____

_____

Sentence #2
(Eliminate the letter *b*.)
Elizabeth bought light brown book covers for all but two of her best books of fiction, and dark blue covers for all her school books.

_____

_____

Sentence #3
(Eliminate the letter *c*.)
Children can create colorful scenes on paper, using only their creativity and basic supplies like watercolors and oils.

_____

_____

Now create some lipogram puzzles of your own to share with the class. Be sure to include a possible solution to each puzzle.

Answer Key
Lipograms

Answers will vary. Here are some possibilities:

Sentence #1:

Rick loved French food, consuming rich desserts often when he visited the country.

Sentence #2:

Liz purchased tan covers for all except two of her favorite novels, and navy covers for all of her school texts.

Sentence #3:

Boys and girls are able to make bright drawings using only their imaginations and ordinary paints.

Holiday Letters

Two holiday messages appear on the grid below. See if you can create words associated with the holidays by adding letters before or after each letter in the messages. You may add any number of letters before or after each existing letter below, so long as you don't run into another word, reading left to right. (You do not need to make words reading top to bottom.) To complete the puzzle, every existing letter below should be part of a new word.

Example

			R	E	D					
C	A	R	O	L	S					
			F	A		L	A		L	A

H
O
L
I
D
A
Y

C
H
E
E
R

H
A
P
P
Y

N
E
W

Y
E
A
R

Answer Key
Holiday Letters

Answers will vary. Here is one possibility:

```
R U D O L P H
            O R N A M E N T S
  T I N S E L
            L I G H T S
      R E D
      C A N D Y
  H O L L Y
                        W R E A T H
            C O O K I E S        C A R D S
  S L E I G H                    P I E
            E V E R G R E E N     P R E S E N T S
      G R E E N                  Y U L E
      T R E E
                          E G G N O G
                              E L F
                              W A S S A I L

                        T U R K E Y
                    M I S T L E T O E
                      N E W   Y E A R S   E V E
                  R E I N D E E R
```

Dictionary Puzzle

elow, one is found in a band, one in a lake and one in a jar.

_____

_____

_____

the word *duped*? _____

3. What do the following words all have in common: *sabot, pump, clog*? _____

   _____

4. Add a letter to the word *shrew* to make a new word that means *cunning* or *tricky*.

   _____

5. Which word doesn't belong in this list: *skiff, tiff, miffed, rift* _____

   Why? _____

6. Can you *pillory* someone by giving them too many pills? _____

   Why or why not? _____

7. Put the words in the following sentence into alphabetical order: *The wicked wizard washed the windows in the wigwam on Wednesday with a washcloth rinsed in windshield wiper fluid.*

   _____

   _____

8. Write one sentence that uses all four of the following words correctly: *shrike, tyke, pike, hike*.

   _____

   _____

9. Could a *milliner* be a *miscreant*? _____

   Why or why not? _____

10. Write one sentence that uses all three of the following words correctly: *euphonious, euphoric, eulogy*.

   _____

   _____

Answer Key
Dictionary Puzzle

1. Pickerel — lake; piccalilli — jar; piccolo — band
2. One
3. All are types of footwear.
4. Shrewd
5. Skiff, because it does not deal with disagreement in any way.
6. No, because *to pillory* means to expose to ridicule and abuse.
7. A, fluid, in, on, rinsed, the, washcloth, washed, Wednesday, wicked, wigwam, windows, windshield, wiper, with, wizard
8. One possibility: *When the tyke took a hike, he saw a shrike and caught a pike.*
9. It's possible. A milliner makes hats. A miscreant behaves criminally or viciously. A hat-maker could be a villain at the same time.
10. One possibility: *The minister's voice was so euphonious during his eulogy that some of the listeners actually forgot their grief and became euphoric.*

Name _____

Happy Trails

Part A

Each four-letter word defined below can be spelled from the letters found in *trails*. The last letter of one answer becomes the first letter of the next answer. You may use the letters as often as you wish, in any order.

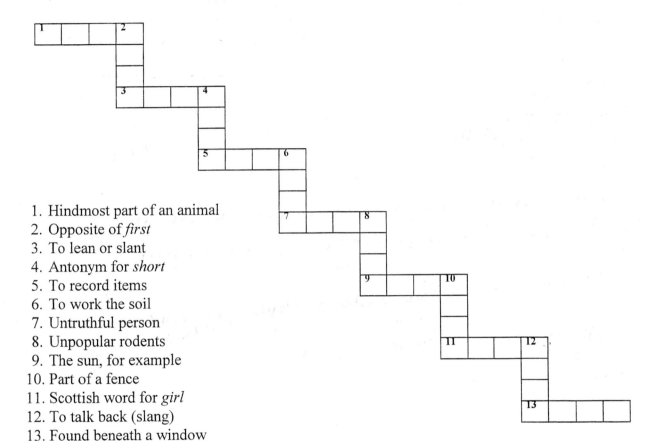

1. Hindmost part of an animal
2. Opposite of *first*
3. To lean or slant
4. Antonym for *short*
5. To record items
6. To work the soil
7. Untruthful person
8. Unpopular rodents
9. The sun, for example
10. Part of a fence
11. Scottish word for *girl*
12. To talk back (slang)
13. Found beneath a window

Part B

Write five sentences in which the last letter of one word becomes the first letter in the next.

Example

Bob borrowed Diane's skateboard.

Answer Key
Happy Trails

1. tail
2. last
3. tilt
4. tall
5. list
6. till
7. liar
8. rats
9. star
10. rail
11. lass
12. sass
13. sill

Summer Vacation

There are many, many common words that can be formed from the letters in the words *summer vacation*. See if you can find the 40 three-letter words that can be used to fill the blanks in the story below.

Remember: You may use only three-letter words, and all the words must be formed from the letters in *summer vacation*. In forming words, you may use a letter more than once in a word *only* if it appears more than once in *summer vacation*.

Summer Vacation Fairy Tale

Once upon a time there was a shy young prince who lived in a kingdom far, far away. Although the prince was shy, he had many talents. He had inherited athletic ability from his Uncle **(1)** _____, a musical **(2)** _____ from his Uncle **(3)** _____, and a way with animals from his Uncle **(4)** _____, who was a **(5)** _____. In addition, the boy was as brave as nine or **(6)** _____ **(7)** _____ put together.

On the summer vacation before the prince's seventeenth birthday, he fell in love. Unfortunately, he fell in love with Princess **(8)** _____, who was not shy at all. The princess neither liked the prince **(9)** _____ disliked him. She simply didn't notice him at all.

The unfortunate prince tried everything to get the princess to notice him. He rented a plane and wrote, "I love you!" in the **(10)** _____ above her castle. She was busy painting a daisy on her big **(11)** _____ and didn't see it.

One night he drove his expensive red **(12)** _____ back and forth in front of the castle, hoping to impress her. However, the princess was too busy waxing her own brand new **(13)** _____ and didn't notice. He swam to her canoe one day when she was fishing in the moat, but she thought he was an alligator and hit him with an **(14)** _____. He put on his jogging shoes and **(15)** _____ past her when she was lying in the **(16)** one afternoon, trying to get a **(17)** _____. But she continued to **(18)** _____ her strawberries and didn't even look up as he passed.

One night he climbed the garden wall, tied a love note to a rock, and tried to toss it into her bedroom window. However, his **(19)** _____ was bad. The rock hit the **(20)** _____ roof of the doghouse below, waking six Doberman pinschers who soon had him on the

(21) _____. He leaped over the garden wall and then **(22)** _____ down with his

heart pounding.

"Nothing I have tried has worked," thought the prince. "I know what does

(23) _____work. Now I need to know what *will* work. I think I will ask my

(24) _____." Immediately, he got up and went to see her.

"**(25)** _____ down, my little Pumpkin," said the queen. She had called him that since

he was a little tyke. "Get your hair out of your eyes," she added, "and **(26)** _____ your

right shoe. I swear, you can never keep a shoe tied." She had talked to him like that since he

had started to walk. She had not noticed her little pumpkin was almost a **(27)** _____.

The prince pushed his hair out of his eyes and tied his shoe. Then he explained his problem.

The queen looked thoughtful. Then she said, "I have **(28)** _____ the princess you

love, and she strikes me as the kind of young lady who would appreciate your athletic ability.

I'll find out when she's going to play tennis with her sister. Then you can arrange to play next

to her, and she will be sure to notice how strong and talented you are."

The next Saturday, the prince set out for the tennis courts on his bicycle. His hair was

freshly **(29)** _____ and combed, and his hopes were high. Unfortunately, his right shoe,

again, was not tied. As he walked out onto the court, he tripped and fell into the

(30) _____.

The prince struggled to his feet, pulled off his shoe, and angrily threw it as far as he could.

Embarrassed at both his clumsiness and his bad temper, he took his jacket off and threw it over

his head. Then he ran, in one stocking foot, to his bicycle.

At last the princess had noticed him. She thought he was some kind of **(31)** _____.

The prince was ready to give up, but his mother was optimistic. "All right, Pumpkin," she

said. "The princess didn't appreciate your athletic ability, but I feel certain that she will

appreciate your musical ability. You must sing for her. Win her heart with a song. You can do it!"

"Well, perhaps I **(32)** _____," said the prince. "I'll even write the song myself!"

Now, while the prince was quite a good singer, he was not much of a songwriter. In fact, he

was a *terrible* songwriter. His song began like this:

You're the one

I love you a ⁽³³⁾ _____.

More than my gun,

Now kiss me, hon.

Then it got even worse.

That night, the prince stood under the princess' window and sang his song. Needless to say, she was not impressed. She threw a shoe at him.

The prince returned, dejected, to his mother. "Don't give up, Pumpkin," she said. "You have one talent left that I'm sure will impress her — your talent with animals. Take your

⁽³⁴⁾ _____ over and dazzle the princess with all the tricks you have taught the animal."

So the prince took his talented feline, Fluffy, over to the castle. He climbed the garden wall and once more stood beneath the princess' window. He had Fluffy walk on her back legs. He had her dance a waltz. When she started slam dancing, even the princess was impressed and came outside for a closer look.

Encouraged, the prince rolled out a ⁽³⁵⁾ _____. Fluffy did a back flip into a cartwheel. The prince pulled out a large tank and filled it. Fluffy danced along the

⁽³⁶⁾ _____, juggling oranges with her front paws at the same time.

Then, suddenly, a mouse ran across the lawn toward the princess. "Charge!" shouted the prince to Fluffy. "Save her! Save the princess!" Fluffy pounced, and in just an instant she held the mouse in her mouth. "It's lucky Fluffy was here," said the prince proudly to the princess.

"Whiskers!" cried the princess, pulling the little mouse from the cat's mouth. "Are you hurt, my poor baby?" She petted the frightened mouse and glared at Fluffy. "You *animal*!" she shouted. "It is a ⁽³⁷⁾ _____ to harm a fellow creature like my Whiskers." She turned to the prince. "And *you*!" She gave him a dark and terrible look. "I never want you to

⁽³⁸⁾ _____ foot on these grounds again! Get out, and stay out!"

The prince left. He never spoke to the princess again. He never spoke to anyone again, all summer long. Fluffy sat around moping, refusing to dance or to do back flips. The queen sat around worrying, trying to figure out why the prince winced whenever she called him "Pumpkin."

Unfortunately, not all fairy tales have a happy ending.

* * * * *

Note: Five years later, the prince ^{**(39)**} _____ a magic marshmallow, which made him get over his shyness. Luckily, princesses all over the world began to notice him. That's where you come in. Tell what happened next, using at least 25 words, each four letters long, that can be made from the letters in SUMMER VACATION. Be sure to underline each of the 25 words you use in your story. Perhaps *your* fairy tale will have a happy ending!

Answer Key
Summer Vacation

Note: There may be more than one correct answer for many of the items.

1. Tim
2. ear
3. Tom
4. Sam
5. vet
6. ten
7. men
8. Sue
9. nor
10. air
11. toe
12. car
13. van
14. oar
15. ran
16. sun
17. tan
18. eat
19. aim
20. tin

21. run
22. sat
23. not
24. mom
25. sit
26. tie
27. man
28. met
29. cut
30. net
31. nut
32. can
33. ton
34. cat
35. mat
36. rim
37. sin
38. set
39. ate

Hearts and Flowers

Sometimes things that are not alike really *do* have something in common, if you look hard enough. For example, you might think that a train and a pizza have nothing in common. Yet both of them involve *chewing*. (You *chew* a pizza, and a train "*choo-choos*.")

See if you can think of at least two similarities between each pair of items below. (Note: There is no single, correct solution to this puzzle. Open up your mind to the possibilities!)

1. How is your heart like a school bus?

2. How is love like an algebra test?

3. How is a bouquet of flowers like a goldfish?

4. How is chocolate like a freckle?

5. How is a valentine like a can of Pepsi?

Answer Key
Hearts and Flowers

Answers will vary. Here is one possible answer for each item:

1. Your heart and a school bus: One *is* a pump, and one *needs* a pump — for gasoline.
2. Love and an algebra test: Both can make you very nervous.
3. A bouquet of flowers and a goldfish: Both need water.
4. Chocolate and a freckle: One can *cause* spots (pimples), and one *is* a spot.
5. A valentine and a can of Pepsi: Both are sweet.

Name _____

Cars

Directions:

For each category listed along the side of the page, think of an appropriate word that begins with the letter at the top of the page. The first item is done for you.

	C	A	R	S
Makes of cars	Chevrolet			
Adjectives that describe cars				
Colors of cars				
Verbs that tell what a car does				
Parts of a car				
Adverbs that tell how someone might drive a car				
Cities in America where you might drive a car				

Answer Key
Cars

Answers will vary, but here is one solution:

	C	A	R	S
Makes of cars	Chevrolet	Audi	Riviera	Subaru
Adjectives that describe cars	cool	awesome	rented	sleek
Colors of cars	cream	avocado	red	slver
Verbs that tell what a car does	careen	angle	race	slide
Parts of a car	Camshaft	axle	radiator	speedometer
Adverbs that tell how someone might drive a car	cautiously	adeptly	rudely	safely
Cities in America where you might drive a car	Columbus, Ohio	Amarillo, Texas	Richmond, Virginia	San Francisco, California

Colors and More Colors

For each item below, study the clue at the left. Write your three-letter answer, in order, in the circles at the right. Then, expand your answer by adding letters to spell out the name of a color.

Example

a falsehood $\underline{O}$ Ⓛ Ⓘ V Ⓔ

1. rock containing metal   ◯ ◯ __ __ __ ◯

2. popular feline pet   __ ◯ ◯ __ __ __ ◯

3. strike   __ ◯ ◯ ◯ __

4. bend at the waist   ◯ __ ◯ ◯ __

5. use a shovel   __ __ ◯ ◯ ◯ __

6. large   ◯ __ ◯ ◯ __

7. young dog   ◯ ◯ __ ◯ __ __

8. small rug   ◯ ◯ __ __ __ ◯ __

9. vine   ◯ ◯ __ __ ◯

10. on the end of the foot   ◯ __ __ __ __ ◯ __ __ ◯

Now see if you can add to the puzzle, writing your clues on the left, below, and leaving the correct number of blanks at the right for each answer. Here are some colors you might start with: lemon, burgundy, lavender, yellow, ebony. (Of course, there are many more.) See how far you can expand the puzzle, and be sure to make an answer key.

Answer Key
Colors and More Colors

1. orange
2. scarlet
3. white
4. brown
5. indigo
6. beige
7. purple
8. magenta
9. ivory
10. turquoise

Diamonds

See if you can complete the diamonds below. Here's how: Add one letter to the letter at the top of each diamond, to make a word. Write that word on the second line of the diamond. Then add another letter to form a new word, rearranging the letters if necessary. Write that word on the third line. Continue to add letters, one at a time, until you can spell the word in the middle of the diamond.

Then take away letters, one at a time, forming a new word each time. When you finish, you should have the same letter that's at the top of the diamond.

Note: There is more than one way to complete each diamond.

Example

```
              O
            O  N
          O  N  E
        D  O  N  E
      T  O  N  E  D
   D  O  N  A  T  E
      A  T  O  N  E
        N  O  T  E
          N  O  T
            T  O
              O
```

```
          A                                 I
        _  _                               _  _
      _  _  _                            _  _  _
    _  _  _  _                         _  _  _  _
  S  T  R  A  I  N                   T  I  N  S  E  L
    _  _  _  _                         _  _  _  _
      _  _  _                            _  _  _
        _  A  _                            _  I  _
```

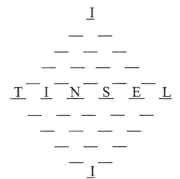

Now create a diamond puzzle of your own, beginning with the letter *E*. You choose the word for the middle of the puzzle.

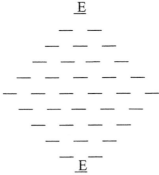

```
              E
            _  _
          _  _  _
        _  _  _  _
      _  _  _  _  _
    _  _  _  _  _  _
      _  _  _  _  _
        _  _  _  _
          _  _  _
            _  _
              E
```

Answer Key
Diamonds

Answers will vary. Here is one solution to each diamond:

```
              A
            A   T
          A   N   T
        T   A   N   S
      S   T   A   I   N
    S   T   R   A   I   N
      T   R   A   I   N
        R   A   I   N
          R   A   N
            A   N
              A
```

```
              I
            I   N
          T   I   N
        T   I   N   E
      S   T   E   I   N
    T   I   N   S   E   L
      T   I   L   E   S
        L   I   S   T
          S   I   T
            I   S
              I
```

The Same, The Same

Many words — and a few names — are spelled the same backward as they are forward. *Pep* and *Anna* are two examples. Can you identify 19 more, below? The definitions and letters will help you.

1. Small child   __ O __

2. Mother   __ O __

3. Make lace   __ A __

4. A joke   __ A __

5. Father   __ A __

6. Past tense of do   __ I __

7. Soda   __ O __

8. Girl's name   __ A __

9. Boy's name   __ O __

10. Worn under chin   __ I __

11. Popular fall flower   __ U __

12. An act   __ E E __

13. Look   __ E E __

14. Blow horn   __ O O __

15. A turning part   __ O __ O __

16. Even   __ E __ E __

17. Detects distant objects   __ A __ A __

18. More red   __ E __ __ E __

19. To direct to a source   __ E __ E __

20. The letters in one of the items above can be switched about to spell a boy's name. It, too, is spelled the same forward as backward. What is the name? _____

21. Add a letter to each pair of *e*'s below to make more words that are spelled the same backward and forward:

     E __ E   E __ E   E __ E   E __ E

Answer Key
The Same, The Same

1. TOT
2. MOM
3. TAT
4. GAG
5. DAD
6. DID
7. POP
8. NAN
9. BOB
10. BIB
11. MUM
12. DEED
13. PEEP
14. TOOT
15. ROTOR
16. LEVEL
17. RADAR
18. REDDER
19. REFER
20. OTTO
21. EYE, EKE, EVE, EWE

Sports

See if you can complete the puzzle on the next page, using words from the world of sports. One letter in each word has been filled in for you.

The clues to the puzzle are not numbered. If the word you want is six letters long and runs across, look under *Across, Six-Letter Words*, for a clue. One of the clues in that column will refer to the word you are looking for.

Across

Three-Letter Words
A small peg
Used to hit a ball
Run
A baseball score

Four-Letter Words
Baseball glove
A basketball needs one
To hit without swinging
Played on horseback

Five-Letter Words
Almost a strike
Baseball throw

Six-Letter Words
They prevent slipping
Tara Lipinski, for example
Done in the Rockies and Alps
Baseball judge
Played on the field or on the ice
The objective in bowling

Seven-Letter Words
Necessary in a marathon
On the forward line
A pole is needed

Words with 8 or More Letters
Court game
Shaquille O'Neal plays
When the band plays
Sometimes transportation for kids
Positioned behind the line of scrimmage
Sports shoes
Football score
Great for flips

Down

Three-Letter Words
Needed in volleyball
To strike
Football player

Four-Letter Words
Type of kick
Done with the foot
You need clubs for it
The "swan," for example
First or third, for example
You do this in water
Throw

Five-Letter Words
Players don't want to be there
Helpful in skiing or fishing
English football
Legal interference

Six-Letter Words
Net game
Soccer or hockey defender
Oars are necessary

Seven-Letter Words
A mask is needed for this position
Swords or foils are needed
To grapple

Words with 8 or more letters
Don't jump out of a plane without one
Kind of bars for gymnasts
Net game
Played on a diamond

Sports Puzzle

To be used with previous page.

Answer Key
Sports

Pluses

Each item below begins with a letter that is followed by a definition for a word. Identify the word and add the letter. Then arrange the letters to spell a noun that we can eat. The first item is done for you.

Pluses	Foods

1. **A** + another word for boys. (*lads*)   s a l a d

2. **O** + a verb that means *to have life*. (_____)   __ __ __ __ __

3. **M** + the name of a beverage. (_____)   __ __ __ __

4. **P** + a verb that means *to jump*. (_____)   __ __ __ __ __

5. **R** + a slang word that means *to arrest*. (_____)   __ __ __ __ __

6. **C** + Raggedy Ann's friend. (_____)   __ __ __ __ __

7. **C** + a word that means *to be wary*. (_____)   __ __ __ __ __ __

8. **C** + a verb that means *to take action*. (_____)   __ __ __ __

9. **B** + a golf term. (_____)   __ __ __ __

10. **C** + the name of bees' homes. (_____)   __ __ __ __ __ __

11. **B** + a term of affection. (_____)   __ __ __ __ __

12. **E** + a math term. (_____)   __ __ __

Now see if you can add five items of your own to the puzzle. Use the space below for your definitions and blanks.

Pluses	Foods

13.

14.

15.

16.

17.

Answer Key
Pluses

1. (lads) salad
2. (live) olive
3. (tea) meat
4. (leap) apple
5. (nab) bran
6. (Andy) candy
7. (leery) celery
8. (do) cod
9. (tee) beet
10. (hives) chives
11. (dear) bread
12. (pi) pie

Word Spirals

To make a word spiral, first choose a topic. Topics are limited only by your imagination. Here are just a few ideas: *animals with four legs, foods that have seeds in them, action verbs, six-letter words, names of people in this class, football teams, words with "x" in them.*

Make a list of all the words you can think of that fit your topic. Then see how many words you can fit into the spiral, printing one letter per square. The last letter of the first word becomes the first letter of the second word. The last letter of the second word becomes the first letter of the third word, and so forth.

Be sure to check your spelling. If you spell even one word incorrectly, your whole puzzle will be "off." Use a dictionary, and have classmates double-check your work as well.

Example

Topic: Synonyms for *big*

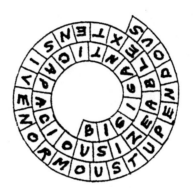

Topic:

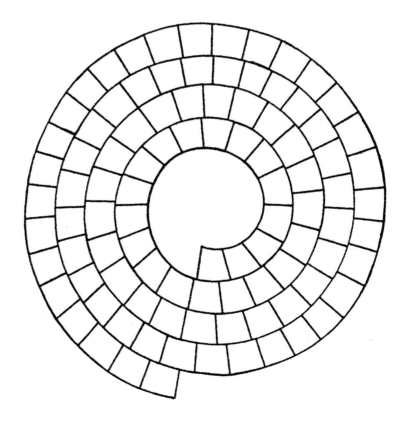

Rhyming Couplets

You may have played this game as "Hink Pink," or you may have heard of it called "Rhymie Stymie." You may have seen a variation on the theme adapted as a game show on TV. Or you may have seen another variation on the old *Tonight Show*, where Johnny Carson played Karnak the Magnificent, a mentalist who furnished humorous questions for the answers first provided by Ed McMahan. Whatever name it goes by, "Rhyming Couplets" is a game that will really stretch your mind.

The basic game rules are simple: You must find the answer to a question, but the answer must be a rhyming couplet — a pair of rhymed words.

Examples

What do you call milk for Bullwinkle? *moose juice*
What do you call mustard and mayonnaise and butter? *spreadable edibles*

Now try your hand at the following rhyming couplets:

1. What would you call a plundered pyramid? _____

2. What would you call an alligator with magical powers? _____

3. What would you call a cheap, preserved cucumber? _____

4. What would you call work at a sword-manufacturing plant? _____

5. What would you call a police body search on a cold night? _____

6. What would you call someone who steals a baby's Huggies? _____

7. What would you call a glass handgun? _____

8. What would you call a summer footwear thief? _____

9. What would you call a father who has just won a million dollar lottery? _____

10. What would you call a problem with flat soda? _____

11. What would you call a person whose hobby is trying to fix broken automobile turn signals? _____

12. What do you call a musician who only works June-September? _____

13. What would you call a foreman in a barbecue condiment plant? _____

14. What would you call an armored bank vehicle? _____

15. What would you call an isolated worker bee? _____

16. What would you call a robot's relatives? _____

17. What would you call D.D.T.? _____

18. What would you call a celebrity limousine? _____

19. What would you call a hospital for pessimists? _____

20. What would you call a wandering Eskimo? _____

21. What would you call an unhappy bowl of hash? _____

22. What would you call the look you get trying to read very small type? _____

23. What do you call a room for holding Japanese currency? _____

24. What do you call a conclusion that's about to happen? _____

25. What do you call a sounding burglar alarm? _____

Now you've got the idea. Next try playing "Rhyming Couplets" in a group. Here are two variations of the game:

A. With a partner see how many rhyming couplet questions you can write. You get a point for each time you stump the class. (Note: The class may come up with a different answer than the one you intended. If the answer rhymes and answers the question, that's fine.)

B. Join one of two class teams. Each team has fifteen minutes to write rhyming couplet questions for the other team. The teams then take turns trying to stump the other.

Answer Key
Rhyming Couplets

1. stripped crypt
2. lizard wizard
3. nickel pickle
4. saber labor
5. brisk frisk
6. diaper swiper
7. crystal pistol
8. sandal vandal
9. happy pappy or glad dad
10. bubble trouble
11. blinker tinker
12. summer drummer or summer strummer
13. sauce boss
14. buck truck
15. lone drone
16. tin kin
17. bug drug
18. star car
19. cynic clinic
20. polar stroller
21. blue stew
22. print squint
23. yen den
24. impending ending
25. crime chime

Name _____

Food for Thought

The English language often uses the names of foods in everyday expressions. For example, cool and damp hands are called *clammy*, or a person who shows fear is sometimes called a *chicken*. See if you can determine the food-related word or phrase that fits each definition below. There are hints at the bottom of the page, if you need them.

1. A phrase used to describe something very simple to do (two answers) _____

   _____

2. A phrase used to describe someone who is very pleased (two answers) _____

   _____

3. Sometimes used to describe a pretty girl's skin _____

4. A short person (two answers) _____

5. A complaint _____

6. Refusing to talk anymore _____

7. Used to describe someone a little bit crazy or crazy-acting _____

8. Making the grade; living up to a certain level of performance _____

9. A phrase to describe something practically worthless _____

10. A car that has everything go wrong with it _____

11. A cherished, special person _____

12. A wimpy person _____

13. To worry and fuss and be angry _____

14. To cheat or bend the truth a bit _____

15. Money (three answers) _____

16. An appointment _____

17. A person who vegetates in front of the television _____

18. To flatter and praise _____

Hints

Two vegetables • a long-cooking meat and vegetable dish • four fruits • a kind of legume • three seafoods • three desserts • a kind of candy • an "extra" for sandwiches • a meat • something that comes in a shell • two dairy products • used for sandwiches • used to create a basic food.

Answer Key
Food for Thought

1. easy as pie; a piece of cake
2. happy as a clam; pleased as punch
3. peaches and cream complexion
4. shrimp; sprout
5. beef
6. clamming up
7. nutty
8. cutting the mustard
9. not worth a hill of beans
10. lemon
11. apple of one's eye
12. cream puff
13. stew
14. fudge
15. dough; bread; clams
16. date
17. couch potato
18. butter up

In Hiding

The word needed to fill in each blank below is hidden in its sentence. Study each sentence carefully. When you rearrange the letters in the right word, in the right order, you will have the answer.

Example

The teacher was very distressed to discover a _____ in the back row.
(The letters in the word *teacher* can be rearranged to spell *cheater*.)

1. The ladies who joined "Save the World" had high _____ .

2. Smith's lawyers had to hire a detective to find their client's _____ .

3. His words were as sharp as a _____ .

4. Close the door, or that awful _____ will escape.

5. You can't keep this photo, but you may have a _____ .

6. They gave the board _____ powers.

7. You can never do too much for a real _____ .

8. Never plan to store that kind of apple. It's the sort that _____ .

9. Whenever he plays checkers, he _____ each move a dozen times.

10. Keep your arm off that freshly-painted table or you will _____ the finish.

Now write five sentences of your own with hidden words. Remember: You should be able to rearrange the letters in one word to fill in the missing blank.

A. _____
_____

B. _____
_____

C. _____
_____

D. _____
_____

E. _____
_____

Answer Key
In Hiding

1. ladies, ideals
2. hire, heir
3. words, sword
4. door, odor
5. keep, peek
6. board, broad
7. much, chum
8. sort, rots
9. checkers, rechecks
10. arm, mar

E-E-E-E-E-Easy Does It

You are a secret agent who must send an important message to a colleague.

Your Mission

Give a clear description of a person you suspect of passing secrets to the enemy.

The Problem

You and your colleague have agreed that the letter *e* used in any communication between the two of you means, "You are in immediate danger; go into hiding immediately." Because you do not want to convey such an alarming message, you cannot use the letter *e* anywhere in your communication. Furthermore, the message you write must be between 70 and 80 words long — no more, no less. Any message of that length means, "Beware of that person mentioned in this letter; he or she may be working for the enemy."

See if you can complete the mission.

Answer Key
E-E-E-E-E-Easy Does It

Answers will vary. Here is one possibility:

This spy looks tall, but not as tall as you. This spy is not a woman. This spy has short light brown hair with a touch of gray. This man has a tattoo of a black scorpion on his right arm. This spy has on a gray wool coat with tartan plaid lining. His tan cowboy boots look old. This man is a musician and has a guitar with him. This spy has a diamond ring on his pinky.

79 words

More resources from Cottonwood Press

TWISTING ARMS
TEACHING STUDENTS HOW TO WRITE TO PERSUADE

We've had so many requests over the years for a book on persuasive writing. Now, at last, we have one we are delighted to introduce. Just a few of the subjects addressed in the book:

- Fact vs. opinion
- Avoiding wishy-washy terms
- Aristotle's three modes of persuasion
- Plagiarism
- Using transition words
- Both traditional and new propaganda techniques
- Writing and supporting a thesis statement
- Ways to provide evidence

Twisting Arms is a practical, engaging book of activities that will help your students learn to write much more effectively. Grades 8-12. Dawn DiPrince. Reproducible. 138 pages.

Order #PHS-B. $21.95

PHUNNY STUPH
PROOFREADING EXERCISES WITH A SENSE OF HUMOR

Your students will really pay attention when you use *Phunny Stuph*. Jokes and humorous urban legends make up all 100 proofreading exercises in this useful book. Use the exercises as transparencies to start class, or photocopy them to pass out to your students.

The errors include a little bit of everything—missing punctuation, spelling mistakes, errors in usage, sentence fragments, and more. Each exercise includes teaching notes and an example of a possible correction. Most exercises are short—just right for quick, frequent lessons that will really help your students improve their skills. Grades 7-12. M.S. Samston. Reproducible. 92 pages.

Order #TA-B. $16.95

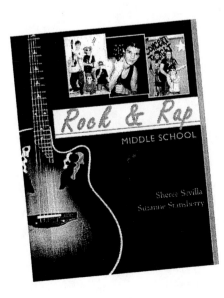

ROCK & RAP MIDDLE SCHOOL

Students learn and have fun at the same time with *Rock & Rap Middle School*. Teachers Suzanne Stansberry and Sheree Sevilla share their highly successful cross-curricular project for middle school students. Students form "bands" and then plan and organize a concert tour, choosing an itinerary, researching the destinations, planning publicity, and much more. Although the activities concentrate on language arts and social studies, the authors include ideas for incorporating *Rock & Rap Middle School* into other subject areas as well. Grades 6-9. Reproducible. 56 pages.

Order #ROCK-B. $12.95

Teaching the Boring Stuff Package

This popular series teaches the basics, but with flair. The books use clever illustrations, humor, and explanations that make sense to young people. Order the books separately, or get the whole package of four books at a 15% savings. Grades 5-9. Reproducible.

Set of four books – **Order #TB4-B. $43.95**

Commas. Teaching students to use commas correctly, without boring them to tears. Randy Larson. 78 pages.

Order #COM-B. $14.95

Quotation Marks. Teaching the basics about quotation marks, without putting students to sleep. Susan Collins. 47 pages.

Order #Q-B. $12.95

Capitalization. Teaching correct capitalization to kids who aren't crazy about writing in the first place. C. M. Thurston. 47 pages.

Order #CAP-B. $12.95

How to Avoid English Teachers' Pet Peeves. Helping students improve their writing by eliminating the common errors that English teachers see most often. C.M. Thurston. 167 pages.

Order #PET-B. $10.95

Interested in something that will really motivate your students? Try our new *Rap-Rap-Rapsody* CD, a set of 25 hip-hop rhythm tracks for the classroom. **Rap-Rap-Rapsody** provides the music. Your students provide the lyrics!

The CD comes packaged with ideas for classroom activities. Have your students create a "Helping Verb Rap," a "Romeo and Juliet Balcony Scene Rap" or a "Spelling Rule Rap," for example. Or use it as part of your poetry unit. The possibilities are endless. For all ages. Music and sequencing by Jay Benedict Brown. 25 tracks. Approximately 66 minutes.

Order #RAP-B. $15.95

To Order More Copies of

Games for English and Language Arts

Please send me _____ copies of *Games for English and Language Arts*. I am enclosing $18.95, plus shipping and handling ($6.00 for one book, $1.00 for each additional book). Colorado residents add 64¢ sales tax per book. Total amount: $_____.

Ship to:

Name _____

School _____
(Include only if using school address.)

Address _____

City _____ State _____ Zip Code _____

Phone _____

Method of Payment:

❑ Payment enclosed ❑ Visa/MC/Discover ❑ Purchase Order (must be attached)

Credit Card# _____ Expiration Date_____

Signature _____

Cardholder Name _____

Cardholder Billing Address *(if different from shipping address)*:

Address _____

City _____ State _____ Zip Code _____

Cottonwood Press, Inc.
109-B Cameron Drive
Fort Collins, CO 80525
1-800-864-4297
www.cottonwoodpress.com
Visit web site for complete product list.
View sample pages.
Order online.
Sign up for free activity every month!